Intersections of Life

ETHEL PIERCE

PAGE PUBLISHING
Conneaut Lake, PA

First originally published by Page Publishing 2023

ISBN 979-8-88654-906-5 (pbk)
ISBN 979-8-88654-916-4 (digital)

Printed in the United States of America

CONTENTS

ACKNOWLEDGMENTS

I would like to thank all the people who believed and inspired me to write these words of inspiration. I would like to especially thank my sister Loretta who was always there for me with words of encouragement.

HATH THOU FORSAKEN ME

Lord, Lord, hath thou forsaken
me, I, your merciful servant
in the midst of my storm?
He who writes such sweet
songs for the songbirds to
sing
He who calms the raging
sea in the midst of the
storm
He who charts the path of
the mighty river
He who divides the dry
land from the wet water
He who created the highest
mountain and the lowest valley
He who speaks to the clouds
and causes the rain to fall
He who takes the mightiest
hurricane and reduces it to
a gentle rain
He who takes the angry wind
and causes it to be still
He who separates the sound
of thunder from the flash
of lightning
He who breathes the breath
of life into every living
creature
He who lets the sun rise
early in the morning and
set late in the evening

He who causes the stars
to twinkle in the darkness
of night
Lord, Lord, hath thou
forsaken me, I, your merciful
servant in the midst of
my storm, or is it I who
hath forsaken thee in the
midst of my storm.

THE BES OF A SERVANT

Be a good servant
Be an honest servant
Be a trustworthy servant
Be a kindhearted servant
Be a loving servant
Be an obedient servant
Be a caring servant
Be a righteous servant
Be a compassionate servant
Be a sincere servant
Be a forgiving servant
Be a gentle servant
Be not a deceitful servant
Be not a judgmental servant
Be all these things so
that no man can speak ill
will of you and declare himself
a Saint before the Master
who is in heaven.

FATHER, FATHER

Father, Father, how I adore
thee
Father, Father, how I love
thee
Father, Father, how I need
thee
Early in the morning when
the sun first rises for
me
In the noon of day when
my way is less certain
Late at night when darkness
surrounds me
Father, Father, how I have
need of thee when the
sun rises and sets more
slowly for me
Father, Father, how I need
thee most, when I have
more yesterdays and fewer
tomorrows.

THE LORD IS MY ROCK

For the Lord is my rock,
in him shall I find my
shelter.
For the Lord is my rock,
in him shall I find my
strength.
For the Lord is my rock,
in him shall I find my
inner peace.
For the Lord is my rock,
in him shall I find mercy
and grace.
For the Lord is my rock,
in him shall I find my
comforter.
For the Lord is my rock,
in him shall I find my
salvation.
For the Lord is my rock,
in him shall I place all
my hope and trust.
For the Lord is my rock,
in him shall I find my
safe haven.
For the Lord is my rock,
in him shall I find my
resting place.

BE A LOVING PERSON

Be a loving person, who loves
each and every person that
you meet along life's divided
highway.
Be a loving person, who hates
no man, woman, or child.
Be a loving person, who gives
not into grief nor worldly
temptations.
Be a loving person, who keeps
the peace when there is war
around you.
Be a loving person, who judges
no man unjustly.
Be a loving person, who is
kind and gentle always.

THE VICTORY

I shout just because, I
am happy for the victories
no matter how large or
how small.
I sing just because, I know
what it means to have
insurmountable joy within my
soul.
I run just because, I have
been set free from the
shackles that held me captive.
I cry just because, I am
so thankful for what the
Lord has done for me.

THE LIGHT

I shall praise thee, O Lord,
while the sun still shineth
bright for me, your faithful
servant.
So that when the storm clouds
of life seek me out I will
not tremble in fright because
I am temporarily blinded from
the light.
I shall praise thee, O Lord,
during the darkness of night,
for the light I seek shineth
brighter than the light from
the sun.
O Lord, did not thou create
the sun and all the brightness
that shineth from the
sun.
Therefore, why must I fear
the darkness if I am a
faithful servant of thee, O Lord,
who is in charge of the
darkness as well as the light
that shineth bright.

THE LORD IN PRAYER

When the struggles of
life become unbearable, I
go to the Lord in prayer.
When sickness comes unto
my bed, I go to the Lord
in prayer.
When trouble comes into my
life, I go to the Lord
in prayer.
When the battles of life
seem to overtake me, I
go to the Lord in prayer.
When I can endure no
more, I go to the Lord
in prayer.

THANK YOU

Thank you, heavenly Father,
for letting me wake up
to a new day of amazing
skies so blue.
Thank you, heavenly Father,
for letting me see another
rising of the sun and the
setting of the same.
Thank you, heavenly Father,
for letting me hear the
chirping of the birds as
I awaken to a brand-new
day.
Thank you, heavenly Father,
for letting me glance upon
the stars and moon before
I close my eyes at night.
Thank you, heavenly Father,
for letting me be able to
appreciate most of all
the precious gift of life.

CRY NOT

Cry not for treasures
that are of this world,
but live so that you
may have treasures in
heaven.
Cry not bitter tears
because others have deceived
you, but pray so that
you may not be denied
your reward in glory.
Cry not because you can
no longer trust others,
but pray so that your
faith in God remains
strong.
Cry not because others have
wronged you, but pray
so that all wrongs are
made right.

GOD ANSWERS PRAYERS

When sickness comes unto
your bed, it shall be mercy
that will bid you to rise.
When sadness comes into
your sickroom, it shall be
unspeakable joy that will
lift you up.
When loneliness comes into
your sickroom, it shall be your
faith that will comfort you.
When death knocks upon
your sickroom door, it shall
be grace that will answer.
When you breathe your last
breath in your sickroom, it
shall be grace and mercy that
will watch over you.

THE LORD DELIVERS

When the Lord has
heard my silent prayer
and has answered my
plea and has delivered
me unto death's door, cry
not for me.
Please know that I have
lived my life according to
thy will and therefore
I need not fear death.
So, my beloved, shed not
bitter tears but let your
tears be tears of joy.
Know in your heart that
I am with my father
standing at heaven's golden gate.

THE COMFORTER

Who shall comfort me
when I am all alone
during my midnight hour?
It shall be thee, O Lord.
Who shall comfort me when
my grief becomes unbearable?
It shall be thee, O Lord.
Who shall comfort me when
my tears become uncontrollable?
It shall be thee, O Lord.
Who shall comfort me
when all my friends have
turned away from me
during my hour of need?
It shall be thee, O Lord.

BE WITH THE LORD

Walk with the Lord
thy God during the
early morning hour.
Talk with the Lord
thy God during the
noon of day.
Pray unto the Lord thy
God at night just before
you close your eyes, then
rest in peace knowing
that the Lord thy
God will keep and protect
you all through the night.

LORD, GUIDE MY STEPS

When I am lost and all
alone and can no longer
find my way in the world,
I pray, O Lord, that
thou will guide my steps
less I stumble and fall,
Lord, guide my steps especially
when my steps become more
difficult and uncertain as
I near the end of my
journey.

THE CLEANSING

Lord, please create in
me, your merciful servant,
a clean heart and
spirit that is pure.
Lord, let my thoughts and
my deeds be kind.
Lord, let my walk be both
righteous and spirit-filled.
Lord, let my talk be like my
walk, loving and comforting.
Lord, let me be a helpful
servant unto them who
need a helping hand along
the way.

TRUST IN THE MASTER

When you find yourself
walking all alone in the
world and friends and
friendships are long gone,
give thanks unto the
master for friends and
friendships that he and
he alone brought into
your life.
Let not vengeance nor
sadness take away your
faith in the master.
Remembering always in your
heart that he and he
alone is still worthy of
all the praise.

THE INVISIBLE

To believe in someone you
cannot see
To trust in someone you
cannot see
To place your faith completely
in someone you cannot see
To totally love someone
you cannot see
To walk tirelessly with someone
you cannot see
To pray without ceasing
to someone you cannot see
Is to know that the Lord
is always with you.

MEMORIES

Cherish not the memories
of so long ago, for they
shall become old and
tarnished with time.
Dwell not on those small,
unimportant things such
as flowers and candy, for
they shall vanish with time.
Hold not on to the sorrows
of yesterday, for those things
are done.
But look toward the heavens
for that which is assured
and everlasting with a
promise of tomorrow.

TREASURES

Look not to treasures of
this world for happiness
for earthly treasures surely
come and go, but look to
the heavens for treasures
that are everlasting.
Look not to treasures of
this world with all their
brightness and glitter, but
look to the heavens for
treasures that are forever
radiant.
Look not to treasure of
this world to last forever
for treasures of this
world may not last, but
look to the heavens for
treasures that are steadfast.

LET NOT

Let not your heart be troubled
by the doings of wicked men
Let not your faith be
shaken by those who
seek to mistreat you
Let not evil men deceive
you into doing those things
that you know to be
contrary to the teachings
of the Lord thy God
Let not earthly greed
separate you from the
Lord's kingdom and all
its richness
Let not the problems of
this world cause you to
grieve needlessly
Let not bitter tears
blind you from the light
which shines from heaven
on high
Let not feelings of loneliness
be your constant
companion
Let not thieves break
in and rob you of your
joy
Let not hatred of any
kind prevent you from
giving the Lord thy
God all the praise.

RICHNESS

It is good to be rich but
unless you can identify
with them who are poor
what does wealth profit
you?
It is good to have untold
wealth, but unless you
are willing to share with
them who are poor, what
happiness does wealth
bring you?
It is good to count your
worldly wealth day to
day, but unless you know
whom to thank and give
praise unto, you count
your wealth in vain.

HE IS ABLE

I shall forever place my
trust in the Lord thy
God.
He who is able to forgive
all my acts of transgression
no matter how large or
how small
He who is able to show
me kindness and love
unconditionally
He who is able to judge the
just and unjust justly
He who is able to wipe
away my tears and ease
my fears
He who is able to look
beyond the outer me and
see the inner me
He who is able to heal my
broken body and make it
whole
He who is able to bring
me through from day to
day.

THE LORD WILL COMFORT YOU

When you feel as if you
are all alone and there
is no one to comfort you
and ease your pain,
Simply fall down upon your
knees and give praise in
earnest unto the heavenly
father and know in your
heart that he hears your
prayer and that he shall
be a comforter unto you.

THE VISITOR

As I sat weeping all
alone during my midnight
hour, I heard a tap upon
my door and in my moment
of despair bid whomever to
enter. Not a word was
uttered by the visitor as
he entered and sat down
next to me. I was feeling an
emotion I did not quite understand
and began to tell the
visitor all about my troubles.
Yet not a word was spoken
as he listened to me tell
about my troubles. All night
and day he stayed with
me as tears ran freely down
my face and a feeling of tiredness
entered into my weary
body.
I must have fallen asleep
for when morning came, I
found myself all alone. I
thus wondered if I in my
moment of despair had imagined
the tap upon my door.

SOMETIMES

Sometimes it seems as
though you travel through
this life all alone and
you think that your problems
cannot be solved and then
you think to yourself, life
is not worth living.
Do not despair and please
do not give up on life but
trust in the Lord with
all your heart, mind, and
spirit to brighten up your
day with friends
yet to come your
way.

I SHALL NOT

I shall not thirst for
the Lord has promised
to provide me with drink.
I shall not hunger for
the Lord has promised
to provide me with food.
I shall not want for
shelter for the Lord has
promised to house me.
I shall not fear the
dark of night for the
Lord has promised to
provide me with light.
I shall not fret over
my tomorrows for the
Lord has promised to
bring me through.
I shall not worry over
that which is unknown to
me for the Lord has
promised to make everything
known to me.
I shall not want for any
thing for the Lord has
promised to provide me with
everything I need from
day to day.

YOUR STORM

No matter the storm
in your life it shall
remain but for a little
while.
No matter how dark the
clouds during the beginning
of the storm they too
shall last but for a
little while.
No matter how hard the
wind blows during the
midst of the storm it
too shall last but for
a little while.
So therefore when trials
and tribulations come
your way, remember the
storm and hold firm
to your faith in he
who controls the storm.

THE BANK OF THE RIVER

As I knelt down to pray
all alone near the bank
of the river, I began to
look back over my yesterdays,
thus my heart became
heavy.
As I lifted my eyes toward
the heavens, I
noticed the dark clouds,
I became even more
troubled as I looked further
back over my life, thus
I began to wonder if I
had been a good and
faithful servant unto
my master. I wondered
had my walk been as
spiritual as it ought to
have been. Then I became
even more troubled over
my tomorrows, would they
be as my yesterdays filled
with sorrow and uncertainty.
Then I noticed for the
first time the movement
of the grass around me,
the beauty of the
flowers surrounding me,
the sun beginning to
break through the clouds.
Then I began to pray
from deep within my heart.
As I prayed, a feeling

of happiness came over
me. Such a joy I began
to feel as a feeling of
peace entered within me.

CROSSING OVER

Lord, there is a river that
each of us shall cross
over.
Lord, how we cross over this
river shall be a testament
of how we have lived our
lives according to your
holy word.
Lord, I pray that my crossing
over to the other side
of the river will be one
of great joy and peace.
Lord, let them that re-
main behind not forget
to praise your sweet
holy name
until they too
are called to cross over
to the other side of
the river.

WHEN YOU ARE GOING THROUGH

When you do not understand
all that you
are going through and it
seems as though you are
all alone,
Let not your heart be
hardened, when it
seems as if the dark
clouds of life are destined
to follow you and you
fall down upon your knees
and ask of the Lord
thy God, why me, O
Lord, and it seems as
though the Lord answers
you not.
Let not this hour of despair
harden your heart against
the Lord thy God. But
renew your faith in him
who knows all that you
are going through.

PROBLEMS

Know in your heart that when
you kneel down to pray that
all your problems can be resolved,
if you honestly believe in your
heart that there are no problems
on this earth that the Lord
cannot solve, if you but wait
patiently and happily on the
Lord to solve your problems,
trusting in him with all
your mind, body, and soul.

FAITH

Step out this day on faith
believe in the Lord thy God
with all your heart. Know
that he can provide all
the answers no matter
how difficult the situation.
Therefore, when it seems that
you cannot make it,
may you learn to trust
in the Lord thy God.

WHEN NOTHING IS LEFT

When you have lost everything
that is dear unto you and
nothing seems to comfort
or console you and the
reassurance of family and
friends is of little comfort
to you.
Please do not hesitate to
give the Lord thy God all
the praise.
Praise him most when all
hope is lost and you find
it impossible to cope.
Praise him in spite of everything
that you have lost
for he alone can give you
the strength to overcome
that which seems impossible
to overcome.

FEEL NOT SORROW

When pain and suffering
come into your life and
certainly they will, please
do not feel dismayed
but simply fall down upon
your knees and give praise
unto the Lord.
Praise him with your whole
heart, and if you must cry,
cry not out of self-pity
but let your tears be tears
of joy.
Remembering that the Lord
hath given you the most
beautiful gift of all, the
gift of knowing that he
is a healer if you keep your
trust in him.

GIVE PRAISE

Praise the Lord thy
God with all your heart
and spirit
Praise him, when your body
is broken and in need of
healing
Praise him when the dark
clouds enter into your life
and you think the sun will
never shine again
Praise him when you are
filled with great sorrow
Praise him, praise him,
praise him always.

THE FOUNT

For so long I have searched
for the fount
I wonder if it exists for me
oh, to find the fount filled
with water that is so pure
and blessed
Oh, to drink from the fount
that is so sweet until
I thirst no more.

BLESS ME, O LORD

Bless me, O Lord, as I
strive to do your will.
Bless me, O Lord, in
your own special way.
Bless me, O Lord, as I
try to do those things you
would have me to do.
Bless me, O Lord, as I
go from day to day with
only nice things to say along
the way.

PRAISE

Praise be unto the Lord thy
God for he watches over
me, thus he protects me in
the presence of my enemies.
He reveals unto me in his
own special way my enemies.
Enemies that are known and
those that are unknown unto
me.
Thus he prepares me to face
my enemies as they line
up against me, and when
it appears that I shall
fall in the midst of my
enemies never to rise again.
You, O heavenly Father, make
your presence known unto me.

THE BLESSED STREAM

Blessed is the stream
that flows through the
rocks.
Holy, holy is the water
that flows from the
stream that flows through
the rocks.
Pure is the water that
flows from the stream
that flows through the
rocks.
I dare not place my
unclean feet within the
stream that is so blessed.
Therefore I bend down
upon my humble knees
and with my hands extended
I thus receive my portion.
I touch my dry lips with
the cool water then drank
more eagerly as I seek
to fulfill my thirst.
As my thirst subsides,
I cry out holy, holy, holy
blessed is the water
that flows from the
stream that flows through
the rocks.

LEST I FORGET

Let me keep my eyes
lifted toward the heavens
lest I forget where my
help cometh from.
Let me stay kneeling upon
my humble knees lest I
forget to praise thee who
giveth me strength
from day to day.
Let me always remain a
faithful and humble servant
lest I forget who is master
and who is servant.

FEELINGS

Let not personal feelings
cause you to do those things
that you know in your
heart to be unjust.
Let not personal feelings
of bitterness prevent you
from seeking the truth
and then accepting it.
Let not personal tragedy of
any kind cause you to doubt
the goodness, grace, and mercy
of the Lord thy God.
Let not personal sorrows
and troubles of this world
prevent you from kneeling
down upon your knees and
giving the Lord thy God
all the praise.

IF IT WERE NOT

If it were not for the storm
clouds that have entered
into my life,
I would not be thankful for my
days of sunshine without rain.
If it were not for my sick
days that seem to last for-
ever,
I would not be thankful for
my days without pain.
If it were not for the turmoil
that enters into my life from
day to day,
I would not be able to appreciate
my days of peace and
tranquility.
If it were not for the days of
sadness that I have endured,
I would not know what it
means to have unspeakable joy.

YOU WERE THERE

Lord, Lord, Lord, 'tis I,
your merciful servant, who
calls upon thy holy
name during the early morning
hour, before the sun riseth
and rooster crows in the
distance.
O Lord, 'tis I who beggeth
of thee to be merciful unto
my wretched soul.
O Lord, I remember how
you stayed with me all during
the night as I tossed and
turned, withering in pain
and crying out for death.
Yet you, O Lord, knew
what was best for me, your
merciful servant, and you,
O Lord, sent your angel
of life to watch over me
when I could no longer care
for myself during my darkest
hour.

THE LORD IS WITH YOU

When you seem lost and
seemingly all alone in
the world and your
friends and neighbors
acknowledge you not.
Do not feel sad and
please do not be discouraged
for the Lord thy God
will be with you always.
Please take comfort in
knowing that the Lord
thy God is more than
a friend and closer than
your dearest neighbor, so
therefore, you need not
fear being all alone when
the Lord is ever present
in your life.

NOBODY KNOWS

Nobody knows why I smile,
when there's nothing to smile
about.
Nobody knows why I cry, when
there's nothing to cry about
Nobody knows why I sing,
when there's nothing to sing
about.
Nobody knows why I shout,
when there's nothing to shout
about.
Nobody knows why I clap my
hands, when there's nothing
to clap about.
But then nobody knows what
I went through yesterday.

THE BLIND MAN

Blesseth be the blind man
for he walketh by his faith
in God and not by his sight
before man.
He feareth not the night
for he is surrounded by
darkness.
So he trusteth fully in the
Lord thy God.
If a blind man so believeth
in him whom he cannot
see, what of the man
whom God has blessed with
sight but refuses to see
that which is?

JUDGE NOT

As I walk among them
who I believe to be less
holier than I,
I ask myself who am I
that I may set myself
in judgment of them.
Let me not forget that
I myself am still under
grace and therefore I
myself am being judged
not by man such as
I, but by he who judges
all.

WHEN YOU PRAY

When you pray, let your
prayers come from the heart.
Pray not out of anger nor
bitterness nor out of fear
of your tomorrow but pray
in earnest.
Remembering always in your
heart that when you pray
that you are praying unto
the heavenly Father and that
it is he who hears and answers
all prayers according to
his will and in his own time.

THE GATHERING OF SAINTS

Lord, when the saints gather
at the river's edge, remember
me, your merciful servant.
Lord, when the saints begin
to sing at the river's edge,
please hear my lowly voice
above all others.
Lord, when the saints begin
to pray at the river's edge,
please hear my gentle words
of praise.
Lord, when the saints begin
to cross over to the other
side from the river's edge,
please take my hand and
guide me safely across.

LORD, LORD

Lord, Lord, lead me to the
river where the water is
pure so that I may be baptized.
Lord, Lord, cleanse my body as
you cleanse my heart.
Lord, Lord, let me not depart
the river as I entered with
my heart unclean.
Lord, Lord, let only them who
are cleansed and just hold
on to my hands as I depart
the river lest I falter.
Lord, Lord, let them who doubt
my cleansing retreat back
into the shadows.
Lord, Lord, let only them who
know what it is to be reborn
remain at the river giving
praise unto your holy and
glorious name.

THE LIGHT

Let's not forget that
in what seems to be
your darkest hour that
there is always a light
which shines bright.
When you are consumed
with heartfelt sorrow
let's not forget that
there is joy, if you but
look forward to your
tomorrow with unshakeable
faith in the light which
forever shines bright.
Therefore when tears of
sadness seem deep within
your very soul, let not
your heart be overburdened
with grief for it is promised
that no matter how great
your grief that it will
be brief, if you but keep
your eyes on the light
that always shines bright.

FOR THE LORD

If it were not for the
Lord, where would I, your
child, be?
If it were not for the
Lord, where would mercy be?
If it were not for the
Lord, I could not see.
If it were not for the
Lord, I could not solve the
problems that trouble me.
If it were not for the
Lord, I could not hear words
spoken unto me.
If it were not for the Lord,
my life would be one of
fear.
If it were not for the Lord,
I would not be able to walk.
If it were not for the Lord,
I would not be able to talk.
If it were not for the
Lord, where would I, your
child, be?

LOOKING BACK

Lord, when I sit and
look back over my life,
I realize that you
were with me and never
let me fall.
Lord, there were times
when I should have fallen,
but you held me close
and did not let me fall.
Lord, I used to wonder
why, but now, O Lord, I know
it was because you loved
me when I did not love
myself.

SWEET HOLY SPIRIT

Sweet holy spirit gone
to your heavenly home no
more this earth to roam.
Sweet holy spirit gone
to be with the Lord.
Sweet holy spirit gone on
to your heavenly home.

MERCY

When pain and suffering
come into your life and
you think that you are
all alone in what seems
to be your midnight hour
and you cry out unto the
Lord thy God for mercy
and yet mercy seems to answer you not.
Please do not feel discouraged
for you are never truly
alone for the Lord thy
God is always with you.
Therefore, please remember
that what seems to be
your midnight hour is not
always at the darkest
point of the night but
it may be at a time
when the sun is shining
bright, or it may be during
the noon of day that
you find that you are in your midnight hour.
Know that no matter
the hour the Lord thy
God is with you and that
mercy is never far away.

WEEP NOT

Weep not bitter tears for
me, no matter how great
your sorrow, for I was
never promised tomorrow.
Let not my homegoing
steal away your joy for
did not God who is all
loving and caring promise
that death would come
to every living thing?
Therefore wipe away your
tears and hold on to
God's promise of eternal life.

REST

When you have made peace
with the Lord and your
soul longs for rest,
fear death not, know in
your heart that the Lord
thy God is with you
and that he will never
leave you nor will he ever
forsake you.
Therefore you need not fear
closing your eyes for what
is to be a short time in
the eyes of the heavenly
father.

MY HOMEGOING

When the sun shall
rise and set no more
for me, your gentle servant
O heavenly Father, I ask
that thou will remember
my acts of kindness
I beg of thee, O Lord, to
remember me both in the
days of my youth and in
my days now golden.
O heavenly Father, I ask
that thou would embrace
my family and friends
so that the news of my
homegoing will not be too
sorrowful for them who
are left behind.

DEATH'S KNOCK

When death has knocked
upon my door and I have
answered, cry not for me,
know that in your heart that
I shall always be just
a wondrous smile away
I shall always be just
a gentle touch away
I shall always be just a
tiny hug away
I shall always be just
a lovely song away
I shall always be just a
soft whisper away
I shall always be just a prayer
away.

FLY AWAY

When my work here is
over and I have done all
that I could do and
have lived my life
according to your will,
and the angel
of death has knocked
upon my door, let me
take wings like an
angel and fly away
to glory.

THE RIVER JORDAN

How shall I travel o'er
to the other side of the
river Jordan?
Shall I take wings like an
angel and fly across?
Shall I take wings like the
gentle dove and glide across?
Shall I take wings like the
mighty eagle and soar across?
Shall I take wings like the
graceful swan and float
across to the other side
of the river Jordan?
Lord, Lord, Lord, how shall
I, your merciful servant,
travel across the river Jordan?

NEVER A PROMISE

Weep not bitter tears for
me, no matter how great
your sorrow, for I was
never promised tomorrow.
Weep not bitter tears for
my body that languishes here,
for I was never promised
a life without suffering.
Weep not bitter tears for
things that are inevitable,
for I was never promised
life eternal.

DEATH

When death comes like a
gentle breeze and places
its kiss softly upon your
lips and you hasten to bid
this life goodbye and tears
fall freely down your cheeks,
and the treasures of this
world mean little to you,
pain and suffering
are no more, and with
your last breath you give
a praise of thanks unto
the Lord thy God.
Rest and feel assured
that you shall sleep for
only a little while.

IF I NEVER

If I never see another rising
of the sun
If I never see another setting
of the sun
If I never see another full
moon at night
If I never see another star
twinkle against the midnight
sky
If I never see another flash
of lightning nor hear the roar
of thunder
If I never see another sky
of blue
If I never see another
changing of the seasons
Lord, I thank you for
all the things I have
lived to see.

OH, LITTLE BIRD

Oh, little bird, with your
voice so sweet sing unto
me your song of praise
Oh, little bird, with your
voice so sweet sing unto
me your song of grace
Oh, little bird, with your
voice so sweet sing unto
me your song of places
traveled
Oh, little bird, with your
voice so sweet sing unto
me your song of peace
Oh, little bird, with your
voice so sweet sing unto
me your song of great
joy and happiness.

THE SONGBIRD

There is a song that the
songbird sings, it is a song
not written by man.
There is a song that the
songbird sings, it is a song
not taught by man.
There is a song that the
songbird sings, it is a song
filled with so much praise
that only the Master can
hear.
Master, Master, how wondrous
his name does sound if
something so small as the
songbird can sing praises
unto the Master all the day
long, ought not someone as
large as man praise the
Master all the day long
even the more.

THE EAGLE AND THE DOVE

On my way to glory I
came upon two birds, one
the mighty eagle the other
the gentle dove.
When asked which bird I
would choose to fly me to
glory, I thought unto myself
then glanced upon the two
birds.
Surely the wings of the
mighty eagle could withstand
the rough winds as
it soared toward glory.
Then I looked at the gentle
dove with its small wings
and wondered if it could
withstand the rough winds
as it soared toward glory.
Then I glanced again at
the mighty eagle and thought
of its strength then looked
again at the gentle dove
and thought of its gentleness.
Then I glanced back at
the mighty eagle as it
flinched its wings in
impatience and then I
looked at the gentle
dove as it waited patiently
for me to decide. As I
looked back at the mighty
eagle, I noticed its powerful
wings as it flew toward

glory.
Then I looked to see if
the gentle dove had flown
away also toward glory,
but to my surprise the
gentle dove sat patiently
waiting for me to decide.
Now, I knew which bird
would fly me to glory,
and then I wondered if
the gentle dove has as
much faith in me.

THE LILY IN THE VALLEY

Noticing I was all alone
in the valley with the
lily, I knelt and began
to pray, as I prayed I
felt a presence near me.
The presence was so over-
whelming that I stood and
looked around me, seeing
no one else, I knelt back
down and again began to
pray, as I prayed I began
to feel my soul become
lighter as my burdens began
to float away.
It was such a change
in and around me that
I stood up and looked
around me, seeing no one
else in the valley, I knelt
back down and once again
I began to pray, as I
prayed I felt the presence
of tranquility surround
me, it was such a wonderful
feeling, one that I had
never before experienced.
Noticing the hour late,
I stood and began to
walk out of the valley
as I walked out of the

valley, suddenly I realized
that I was never alone,
for you, O Lord, are
forever present in my
life.

THE LILY WAITS FOR YOU

When you feel all alone
know that there is a
lily in the valley waiting
for you.
Know in your heart that
the lily will take care
of your every need.
Know deep within your
spirit that your burdens
need not be heavy if
you but take hold of
the lily who waits in
the valley patiently for
you.

THE ROSE

Let your life be as the
rose bright and beautiful
ever basking in the early
morning hour
Let your life be as gentle
as the rose petal ever soft
to the touch
Let your life be as the
rose trusting in the strength
of the stem
Let your life be as the
rose made ever so lovely
because of the color of
the leaves
Let your life be as the rose
bringing joy and delight
into the lives of those
it touches along the way

THE LILY

There is not a flower as
lovely as the lily
There is not a flower as
everlasting as the lily
There is not a flower that
has the strength of the lily
There is not a flower that
is as dear to the heart than
the lily
There is not a flower as
worthy of praise than the
lily

DARK CLOUDS

When dark clouds come
into your life and seem
to last forever, please
do not fret and
become discouraged.
Know that the Lord thy
God can remove all the
dark clouds if you are
patient and wait on
him.

THE STORM

Fear not the storm, for the
Lord thy God will see you
through, if only
you but trust in him.
Fear not the storm for it
shall last but for a little
while, but the Lord's grace
and mercy shall last an
eternity if you will only lean
on him when you begin to
go through your storm.

BLESS THE CHILD

Bless the child whose eyes
shine bright with innocence
Bless the child who is trusting
and kind
Bless the child who is punished
unjustly
Bless the child who suffers
from illness
Bless the child who labors
long hours
Bless the child who begs
for food
Bless the child who thirsts
for water
Bless the child who fears
war
Bless the child who sleeps
on the ground
Bless the child who waits
patiently on the Lord thy
God

THE DEATH OF A CHILD

No words of comfort can
take away the pain that
the death of a child
brings.
No amount of tears can
ease the pain that the
death of a child brings.
No gentle embrace can
ease the emptiness that
the death of a child brings.
Only time and undying
faith in the Lord can
bring you through what
is your darkest hour.

THE LOSS OF A CHILD

Who shall comfort the
mother who has lost her
child?
It matters not that the
child was good or bad
for she will be equally
saddened by such a loss.
Who shall wipe away her
tears for it is a mother's
nature to cry?
I dare say it is hard
for her eyes to remain
dry so shaken with grief.
Who shall help her mend
her broken heart for it is
hard for her to understand
such a tragedy?
Who shall help this mother
sleep at night for it is
at night when her burdens
seem heaviest?
It is her faith and her
trust in the Lord thy
God that will see her
through for the loss
of a child is the greatest
loss of all.

A CHILD ON THE ROAD

It is good for a child
to travel slowly down the
road of life and to
follow the directions of
others who know the way.
To do those things that
are not contrary to the
teachings of the Lord
thy God, though it
will take this child a
little longer to get to
the end of the road
of life, this is the way
it should be.

BLESSED BE THE CHILD

Blessed be the child who
cries all alone during the
midnight hour, for who will comfort
him?
Blessed be the child who desires
peace, for who will be his
peacemaker?
Blessed be the child who goes
to bed hungry, for who will
feed him?
Blessed be the child who comes
naked into the world, for who will
clothe him?
Blessed be the child who seeks
after joy, for where lies his
happiness?
Blessed be the child who is
surrounded by hatred, for who
will teach him kindness?
Blessed be the child that is
surrounded by lies, for where
lies his knowledge of truth?
Blessed be the child who
is homeless, for who will give him
shelter?
Blessed be the child who is
surrounded by violence, for who
will protect him and keep
him safe?
Blessed be the child who desires
prayer but is unable to pray,
for who will kneel with him
and teach him to pray?

ABOUT THE AUTHOR

Ethel Pierce attended both Valencia Community College and Florida Technological University, now known as University of Central Florida, where she earned a bachelor's degree in criminology.

She has worked for over thirty-five years as a volunteer at her local elementary school in various capacity. She has also worked for over thirty-five years in retail sales. She often chooses to meditate during her free time.